T0065337

Other Books* by Lisa A. Wisniewski

Chapters
Directions
Seasons
Landscapes
Storms Within
Fences and Walls

*Published by Grelin Press

Nikki Jean

Lisa A. Wisniewski

WESTBOW
PRESS®
A DIVISION OF THOMAS NELSON
& ZONDERVAN

Copyright © 2016 Lisa A. Wisniewski.

All rights reserved. No part of this book may be used or reproduced by any means, graphic, electronic, or mechanical, including photocopying, recording, taping or by any information storage retrieval system without the written permission of the author except in the case of brief quotations embodied in critical articles and reviews.

Scripture taken from the New American Version of the Bible.

WestBow Press books may be ordered through booksellers or by contacting:

WestBow Press
A Division of Thomas Nelson & Zondervan
1663 Liberty Drive
Bloomington, IN 47403
www.westbowpress.com
1 (866) 928-1240

Because of the dynamic nature of the Internet, any web addresses or links contained in this book may have changed since publication and may no longer be valid. The views expressed in this work are solely those of the author and do not necessarily reflect the views of the publisher, and the publisher hereby disclaims any responsibility for them.

Any people depicted in stock imagery provided by Thinkstock are models, and such images are being used for illustrative purposes only. Certain stock imagery © Thinkstock.

ISBN: 978-1-5127-3937-4 (sc)
ISBN: 978-1-5127-3939-8 (hc)
ISBN: 978-1-5127-3938-1 (e)

Library of Congress Control Number: 2016906615

Print information available on the last page.

WestBow Press rev. date: 05/03/2016

In Loving Memory of
Nikki Jean

Epigraph

A faithful friend is a sturdy shelter; he who finds one finds a treasure. A faithful friend is beyond price, no sum can balance his worth. A faithful friend is a life-saving remedy, such as he who fears God finds; for he who fears God behaves accordingly, and his friend will be like himself. – Sirach 6: 14–17

Acknowledgements

I would like to thank the canine companions throughout my life who have provided me with remarkable insight, rich experiences, and great stories; family members and friends for their encouragement, support, and understanding; and God for the many blessings He has bestowed upon my life. Thanks also to WestBow Press for publishing my work.

Introduction

Life is a journey full of relationships, experiences, and perspectives. Our relationships often play a part in our experiences and perspectives. Some relationships take more time and effort than others to flourish. Sometimes relationships are planned, other times they come about naturally or by divine intervention. In either case, a bond is formed. This bond is often tested by life circumstances and events out of our control. How we respond to such tests impacts the strength and integrity of the bond.

The bond between two creatures has the potential to be extraordinary in many ways. This potential is a byproduct of faith, hope, and love. Our faith guides us through the unknown and provides us hope. Faith and hope combine to lead us to love, where we experience the richest blessings in life.

The blessings granted to us through time provide perspective to view the world around us. Though the view may be dismal and dreary on the surface, perspective allows us to see through the gray clouds to the rich, vibrant colors waiting below to be discovered, nurtured, and treasured.

One of the greatest blessings ever bestowed to me was my dog, Nikki. Our relationship formed a bond full of faith, hope, and love. Through this bond, I found a new perspective in which to view life. This perspective became increasingly important in providing strength to endure life's trials and tribulations, and in helping me care for my grandmother later in life. Nikki also helped me to see nature's many wonders and lessons. Because of Nikki, I developed a more intimate relationship with nature and learned to appreciate the little things in life we may take for granted, such as the sunrise, the sky, and even raindrops.

My experience with Nikki leads me to believe that who we know or come to know in our lives plays a part in our understanding, growth, and character. As humans, we naturally need interaction with others. This interaction may be positive or negative in nature, but how we view this interaction is what ultimately impacts us most. To help illustrate my point, I wrote the following poem:

Who We Know

Who we know and how we know them
Are seeds sowed where we have been,
Watered by time and sustained by the sun
In the garden of life where each day begun
Offers opportunities to explore
In the beauty placed before
Us in the art of nature's ways
Spread near and far by the coming
and going of each day.

Who we know and how we know them
Allow us to grow shoots and stems
Emerging from the earth in shades of green
Spreading worth from the seed
That becomes a blossom or a vine
Conveying thoughts that mend and hope in time
To connect with and build upon
As our roots spread out beyond
The weeds and the brush
To fulfill the need in each of us.

Before Nikki entered my life, I was always in a hurry to accomplish tasks and move on to the next item on the to-do list. Though I was experiencing life, I was not really *living* life. Once Nikki came to live with my grandmother and me, I started to recognize that the little things mean the most, and the bigger things are often not all that great once you remove the showy exterior façade.

This story is one I share with the hope it helps others in some way, even if that way is small in the grand scheme of life. Though this story is true, some of the names have been changed for privacy purposes.

Chapter One
Beginning the Journey

Nikki and I met for the first time in April of 2002. It was not a chance meeting, but rather one of those divine interventions that we don't quite understand when it happens. A few weeks earlier, I started searching for a dog for my grandmother. Gram lived next door to me all my life. She lost her beloved German shepherd, Ginger, to hip dysplasia years earlier. My grandfather passed before I was even born. Always very independent, Gram disliked asking for help— although she did enjoy when my cousins, my sister, and I helped her with house and yard work.

As a youngster, I dreamed of someday buying Gram's house and raising my family there. In my teenage years, Gram and I spent a lot of time together. Arthritis left her with some limitations, and as the oldest of her grandchildren, I felt obligated to help with chores she could no longer do. On weekends, my sister and I cleaned the house while Gram cooked in the kitchen. During the week, I walked through the field that separated our houses to check on Gram and do yard work after I got home from school.

As the years wore on, I saw Gram become frustrated with her limitations. She grew somewhat depressed, often lamenting certain situations. Eager to help, I prayed for guidance in finding something to bring Gram out of her saddened state.

One night while reading the paper, the classified ads caught my attention. My eyes fell to the pets section. Honing in on the German shepherd ads, I realized a dog might be the ticket to helping Gram. However, the costs listed and other criteria did not fit either of our financial situations. Not one to be deterred, I went to the computer and got on the Internet to search for other means of obtaining a dog. Dog shelters and rescue groups offered the most reasonable and feasible options. After carefully reading about each dog, I wrote down contact information and got to work emailing or calling about the prospects.

Most of the conversations went something like this:

"Hello. XYZ Shelter/Rescue Organization. How may we direct your call?"

"I am interested in knowing more about Dog ABC (fill dog's name in here) and would like to ..."

"Oh, Dog ABC is already adopted/no longer available (fill in excuse here). Thank you for calling. Goodbye."

After a great deal of calls that led nowhere, I started to think there was some sort of caller ID that lit up and labeled me as an unworthy adoption option when I phoned these organizations. Not sure what else to do,

I prayed to God for help again and again and again: "Dear God, can you please help me with this? I am not sure what I am doing wrong here. I just want to help Gram and can't get anyone else to cooperate."

Then I stumbled across an organization called Chances Pet Rescue. It was local, and from what I read, the owner was sincere about placing pets in loving homes. Taking a deep breath, I dialed the number while on break at work.

"Hello. Chances Pet Rescue. This is Jane. How can I help you today?"

"Hi, Jane. My name is Lisa and I was wondering if you happen to know of any German shepherd dogs in need of a home."

Closing my eyes, I braced myself for the typical response. However, I was caught off guard and surprised when Jane said, "Why yes. Just this morning a young woman called with a four-and-a-half-year-old female German shepherd in need of a home. Can I take your information and get back to you about a time to meet?"

We exchanged details and I hung up the phone somewhat in shock. *This could finally be happening!* was all I could think all day. I ran to Gram's house after work to tell her about the possibility of having a dog in the house again.

Bursting through the door, I said, "Guess what, Gram! I have some good news. You may be getting a dog. Don't worry, I'll help you with the care and any vet bills. Wouldn't it be great to have company when you come home from work?"

I was not prepared for the response I got. Looking at me over the rims of her glasses, Gram said, "Lisa, Lisa. I don't need a dog now. What made you think I needed a dog?"

Sighing deeply, I explained I felt it would help. I also launched into my sales pitch for me to buy Gram's house and have her stay there free of charge.

Gram would not budge. We went back and forth for hours while I did chores and she watched and fussed about the situation. Finally, I said, "Please just agree to meet the dog. The rescue organization may not deem us suitable to adopt her. Please, will you agree?"

"Well, okay. But please don't get us in over our heads with your big ideas," Gram replied.

Jane called the next day to confirm the meeting. She also provided the details of the situation: "The dog's name is Nikki. She is somewhat of a couch potato, but gets along well with other dogs, cats, and children. Her owners, Tim and Mary, are starting a family, and Tim travels a lot. Mary feels she can't give Nikki the attention required. They are both very torn about the situation, but they want Nikki to have a loving home with ample room to run and plenty of things to do."

After listening carefully, I could not help but feel deeply for the young couple and Nikki. How hard this decision must be for them and how much emotional pain they must be experiencing! Swallowing hard, I said, "Jane, I want to help as best I can and I do feel Gram's farm would be a great atmosphere for Nikki. Yes, we will meet with you."

The meeting would not take place for two agonizing days. During that time, I found my mind racing and my body unable to sit still. Concentrating at work was a lost cause. I needed the meeting day to arrive. My impatient side was driving me crazy, as were the number of questions Gram kept asking me:

"Are you sure this dog is a female? I don't want a male dog because they go to the bathroom on everything."

"What kind of dog food are we going to have to buy?"

"Do you think we can use Ginger's old water dish? It's under the kitchen sink next to her old food container."

"Where will she sleep? Ginger always slept behind my recliner or in the bedroom above the kitchen."

"Am I going to have to let her out? You know I can't get up and down the steps very quickly these days."

"What about a license? Will we have to apply for one?"

"Does she have shots? What vet will we use? The vet Ginger had retired."

"Will she run away? You know none of our dogs in the past were runners."

"Do I need to buy dog biscuits when I go shopping tomorrow?"

"Are you sure you can pay for her? You know I don't get paid until next week."

"What about…"

Chapter Two

Intentions and Impressions

Standing in the garage, staring at the rain, and trying not to get ahead of myself, I waited for Jane, Nikki, Tim, and Mary to arrive. The night was cool for April. It was also dreary and gray. Not exactly the picture I had envisioned for a first meeting. I kept looking at my watch and looking through the rain to the edge of the driveway. Every sound echoed in my head. Every car going past made my heart jump into my throat.

Finally, I heard tires hit the gravel in the driveway. First came a small foreign car driven by the woman who introduced herself as Jane. Then a very nice Mercedes rolled up with a woman who I would learn was Mary and a little girl named McKay. Another Mercedes driven by a man I suspected was Tim pulled up last. In the back seat was the most beautiful German shepherd I had ever seen in my life. She peered eagerly out of the window, but she was very well behaved and waited until the car stopped before moving. I felt as if

I was in a dream and would wake up at any moment without knowing the outcome.

Tim opened the car door for Nikki. Like a movie star, she stepped out into the evening air. Her face was dark, mostly black. She had a black saddle that stood out over the tan remainder of her body. Her eyes sparkled with an enthusiasm and eagerness that touched me deep into my core. She was calm, large boned, yet graceful in her movements.

Composing myself as best I could, I approached the group and introduced myself. "Hi. I'm Lisa. Let's get out of the rain and go into the kitchen. My grandmother is waiting there for us."

Entering the house, Tim and Mary both commented on the rustic decor and old-fashioned, down-home feel conveyed by the antique white trim and tin kitchen walls. We sat at the kitchen table. Mary bobbed McKay on her knee. Tim talked about getting Nikki from a breeder and how hard it was for him to be in this position. Jane explained the trial adoption period of two weeks and what the next steps would be if we were to proceed. Gram kept quiet, except to answer questions about the house and how long she had lived there.

A few minutes into the conversation, I felt a nudge at my leg. Since we did not have enough chairs, I opted to stand. Looking down, I saw Nikki leaning against me. She had already made her decision on the matter, unknown to the others. Reaching down, I stroked her neck. Her fur was very soft and warm.

Instantly, I felt calm and reassured. She looked up at me with the most honest, sparkling eyes, and my heart just melted.

As we took turns talking, Nikki moved around the room. She sniffed many of Ginger's old favorite spots and settled by Gram for a while. Gram looked down and gave Nikki a pat on the head. They silently studied each other for some time before Nikki returned to me almost smiling as if to say, "Don't worry. It will be alright."

Her eyes sparkled against her dark face. She was majestic, almost like royal lineage the way she carried herself and exuded a confident aura, but not in a cocky or pompous way. I was mesmerized and almost lost track of the conversation for a few moments. My heart beat steadily in my chest as my head pounded in excitement. I was already under Nikki's spell, although we had just met. It was a spell with which I was familiar since I had lived with German shepherds since I was born. Something about the loyal, honest eyes and huge frames full of energy clicked with me early in life, allowing me to feel secure and able to conquer challenges with these dogs by my side.

After a lot of questions, answers, contemplation, and a little laughter, we decided to allow Tim and Mary to wait a few days before making a decision. I did not ask if other parties were interested, so I had no idea what the odds were of Nikki actually coming to live with Gram. All I knew was Nikki and I had made a connection. I felt this connection was for a reason that only God in heaven could explain.

As the cars pulled out of the driveway into the drizzle of the night, I caught a glimpse of Nikki peering out the window. She looked like a celebrity in a limousine, yet she had this folksy, honest aura with an eager-to-please gaze and intent stare. Our eyes met as if we did not want to say goodbye. At that moment, I prayed to God, asking Him to please make the stars align to fulfill our needs.

Chapter Three
Adopting and Adapting

The next few days were anxious ones for me. I tried very hard not to set myself up for disappointment. Giving up a dog is not easy to do. The only experience I had in this area was when one of my dogs passed away. Whether the circumstances were sudden due to natural causes, like with my first dog, or planned due to severe illness, letting a dog go was an emotional rollercoaster ride. Part of you is trying to be realistic and do right by the dog, and part of you wants to hold on and not let go.

In Nikki's case, it was a big decision for all parties, and the outcome of this decision would be life-altering for everyone involved. In my mind, I tried to keep my thoughts even-tempered and reasonable. In my heart, I just wanted what was right to happen. The only problem was neither my heart nor my mind knew what *would* happen. The waiting left every part of me restless.

After a few days, Jane called to say that Tim and Mary had made a decision. Bracing myself with a deep breath, I listened carefully as Jane said, "Tim and Mary would like Nikki to come stay with Gram. They were very impressed and feel Nikki could not have a better home!"

Part of me wanted to scream *YES!* Another part of me wanted to cry, and still another part of me said I could not stay silent and needed to say something in return to Jane. All I could say was, "Thank you very much."

We agreed to sign the papers and to meet at Gram's house on Saturday, May 4. The meeting would be early in the morning, and all parties would receive final instructions at that time.

In somewhat disbelief, I hung up the phone. I felt as if I had just hit the German shepherd jackpot. My mind raced with things to do to prepare for the big day. Some things I would be able to do before Nikki arrived, like moving furniture in the house to give her space. Other things would have to wait until I had obtained specifics from Tim and Mary, like what type of food Nikki liked and when she was due for shots. I also had to prepare Gram for some changes. Gram and I talked each night about where Nikki would sleep, the possibility of me moving in temporarily to make sure the transition was as smooth as possible (Gram was still adamant about remaining independent), and making the house dog-proof once again.

Saturday dawned clear and bright. I went for my typical morning run, full of energy, hope, and uncertainty for how the remainder of the day would unfold. Gram was a bit moody and not very cooperative. I tried to be patient and understand her viewpoint. This was a huge change for her, which I realized. What I did not realize at the time was her fear of losing independence. In hindsight, I should have handled the matter a bit differently--although I doubt the outcome would have been altered since from the moment Nikki arrived, it was apparent divine intervention would prevail no matter what happened in life.

Jane, Tim, Mary, and Nikki arrived on time. I could not help but notice Tim was holding back tears. It was obvious this was very difficult for him. He had picked Nikki out from the litter himself and had taken her to obedience classes. Mary was also struggling with emotions, but she kept saying that they could not have asked for a better home for Nikki.

We came into the kitchen to sign papers for Jane's records. The papers stated Tim and Mary agreed to turn Nikki over to Gram and me. Jane made sure we understood the wording and the terms listed. She asked Tim to sign first. He hesitated, biting his lip before scrawling his signature quickly across the page and putting his head down. I felt dearly for him, and I looked to Jane and Mary for reassurance before signing my name. Nikki would stay with Gram, but I would be responsible for all vet bills, care, payments, etc.

After signing, I asked Tim and Mary about paying them. It was an awkward moment, for we had not discussed it prior. Although they were giving Nikki up, I thought I had to offer monetary payment for her. The day before, I went to the bank and took money out of my account. As I asked the question, it dawned on me I may not have enough money to cover the cost since Nikki was pure bred and obedience trained. I certainly was not prepared for Tim's response.

"We cannot accept money for her. We feel God sent you to help us, and that is payment enough. We brought her crate, dog bed, feeding dish, leash, and some food to help make the transition easier for everyone."

Now it was my turn to hold back tears. I helped Tim get Nikki's crate out of the car. He showed me how it went together and explained that she liked to go in and out of it as she pleased. If I needed her to go into the crate and stay inside for any reason, all I had to do was say, "Kennel up."

Tim also explained Nikki knew other commands like sit, wait, gentle, and down. She was messy with drinking water, so he cautioned me about making sure her water dish was in a place that was easy to clean. Mary added information about feeding times and quantities of food. She also handed me two bandanas. "Nikki likes to wear these around her neck like the one she has on today. She gets them dirty though, so I have several for her. I wash her bed once a week and put it in her crate. The stuffing comes out and the cover can be thrown in the washer."

I offered again to give Tim and Mary money to cover the cost of Nikki's belongings. They again refused, so I said, "I understand this must be very difficult. Please know you are welcome to visit her at any time. You can call ahead or just stop by if you see us out in the yard. I want you to feel welcome and to continue to be a part of her life, if you are comfortable in doing so."

Tim and Mary looked surprised at my offer, but they were open to visiting. Tim asked, "If anything should ever happen..."

I stopped him in mid-sentence, "Don't worry. I will call you and keep you informed. I promise. It is the least I can do."

We shook hands, and Tim and Mary said they had better leave. They said their goodbyes to Nikki, and they told her she would be staying with Gram and me. Nikki looked a little confused and anxious at first, especially when Tim and Mary pulled out of the driveway without her in the car. She whimpered, but I gently tugged at her leash and knelt down beside her.

"It's okay, Nikki. I know this must be hard for you, too. Please know I'll do my best to be understanding and patient."

We went into the house to see what Gram was doing. I was not prepared for Gram giving me a piece of her mind about having Nikki in the house. Gram made a huge fuss, so I stated I would be solely responsible for Nikki, and that Nikki would be my dog since Gram was suddenly opposed to the idea of owning Nikki. Once again, I did not understand Gram's side of things, but I tried to remain patient.

At that moment, I felt a bit overwhelmed, but something about Nikki's presence calmed me. Somehow this was going to work out for everyone, although the specifics were not clear to me. Thus began what would become a bond in the journey called life that no words can fully describe.

Chapter Four
Challenges of Change

Nikki adjusted quite well—much better than Gram—to her new surroundings and routine. I stayed with her and Gram the first few nights to make things easier and to keep the peace so to speak. Nikki was a very vocal dog, always barking or making little sounds at the door while watching the birds outside. It did not bother me much, but it irritated Gram, and I'm sure the neighbors were not too thrilled with all the noise. Luckily, all the close neighbors at the time were related to us, so they were very understanding.

Gram found reasons to complain each day about something Nikki did. One day, Gram said, "You have to ship Nikki back."

"Why? What's wrong now?" I asked.

"Lisa, I can't explain it. Just ship her back," Gram replied.

"Gram, I can't just give up without knowing why. Everything happens for a reason. Nikki needs and deserves a good home. We can give that to her," I replied.

"Lisa, Lisa. Why do you get us into these things?" Gram asked.

Tim and Mary had placed a lot of trust in me. I was not about to let them down or lose Nikki. No way, no how, no matter what I had to do, I was going to see this through one hundred percent, down to the last detail. Taking a deep breath and mustering up all the courage I had in my twenty-eight--year--old body, I said, "Gram, I'm sorry, but we are all going to have to adjust and get along as best we can."

Much to my relief, Gram softened on the matter. I don't know if this was due to divine intervention, or to Nikki's way of wrapping others around her paw. Whatever the reason, I am forever grateful it occurred.

Soon, Gram was calling all of her sisters and saying, "Guess what? I got a dog. Her name is Nikki. She's a German shepherd. Pure bred. Black and tan. She likes to wear bandanas around her neck..."

All that fuss and now Gram was claiming Nikki. I had to laugh and shake my head at times, for with Gram, you never knew if she was serious or just trying to get her own way. She was used to dictating how things would go pretty much all the time. Few people dared to cross her, for she played the sweet grandmother well, but she could also be the domineering matriarch with a sharp tongue.

Of course, when Nikki did something Gram considered wrong, Nikki suddenly became my dog.

If Nikki barked too much, I got the make your dog be quiet speech. If Nikki spilled water on the floor, it was the clean up after your dog speech.

For me, it was frustrating at times, but I kept telling myself that someday, somehow, all would be right in our world. I gave all I had to Nikki and then some. It was worth the effort. Had I known what the future held, I would have tried to give her even more.

Every day during the week, I got up early to take care of Princess, a German shepherd whom my family adopted in the spring of 1991. Princess lived at my mom's place, and at this point in life, she needed special medicine at each meal for joint issues. Although Princess was the family dog, I had assumed responsibility for her care when I was in my early twenties.

After caring for Princess, I walked over to Gram's house to take care of Nikki, who was always ready for me to let her out and feed her before I left for work. When I came home at the end of the day, I cared for Nikki first, went home to care for Princess, and spent the evenings trying to get Nikki and Princess acquainted. This was not an easy task, for Princess had been an only dog for twelve years, and had received all of my attention. It did not help matters that Nikki barked her head off every time I got within forty feet of her with Princess.

Princess and Nikki could finally be together after about a month of trying to get acquainted. Slowly, they began to play with each other. Both liked to play ball, so I took them into Gram's back yard and threw the ball. Nikki took off after the ball, Princess took off after Nikki, and I followed chasing both of them. Gram watched from her chair on the porch, so everyone was quite entertained.

After Nikki had been with us for about six months, we had our first major incident. I was out in the yard trying to do yard work in the chilly weather. It was starting to get dark, and I was tired. Nikki spotted a cat in the field and took off after it.

"Nikki, NO!" I yelled as I ran after her and the cat.

If I did not catch Nikki before she reached the edge of the fields where the wood line started, I knew I would lose her in the thick brush. I ran as fast as I could, but my boots and heavy coat hindered me. My chest started to burn from gulping the cold air into my lungs. I stumbled a few times in the ruts of the field because my eyes were fixed on Nikki and not on where I was going.

Suddenly, the cat darted under a thorny thicket. Nikki hesitated for a split second, which gave me time to lunge and tackle her to the ground. I tried to be gentle, despite the fact I had hurled myself through a good distance. I'm not sure who was more surprised when we hit the ground. I do know I felt a wave of relief knowing I had not lost her.

"Are you okay, Nikki? I'm sorry I had to tackle you like that, but I just couldn't bear the thought of losing you in the woods," I said as I picked myself and Nikki up off of the ground.

At the time, Nikki weighed about ninety pounds. I led her by the collar all the way up the hill to the house, which was a little over a quarter of a mile. By the time I got her inside, my chest was on fire. Nikki was breathing heavily from her chase. I sat her on the floor by the door and told her in the best adult voice I could muster, "Nikki, if you ever do that again, you are going to give both of us a heart attack."

Chapter Five
Adjusting and Accepting

In late February of 2003, Gram had a fainting spell at work. Gram refused to go to the hospital, so my mom had to go pick Gram up at work and bring Gram home. That night, Mom and I talked at length with Gram about what had happened. We were very concerned and thought Gram should seek medical attention. True to form, Gram would not budge.

Every night I sat with Gram at the kitchen table trying to convince her to let me move in permanently. I offered to pay all the bills and take care of any repairs to try to make the proposal more appealing. Gram held her ground, and we went around and around debating each night. Finally, Gram gave permission for me to move in permanently.

On March 1, 2003, I moved into the bedroom above the kitchen, which was my mom's room as a teenager. I felt free and independent in a way I had not experienced before. Nikki followed me up and down the steps for every trip I made while moving my belongings into the house. Her eyes sparkled, and she had a smile on her face like when we first met.

"Are you happy, Nikki?" I asked as I ruffled her soft fur with my hand.

Oh, how she could read my thoughts and feelings so well! I could not have asked for more at this point in my life.

Nikki was so tired that night, she fell asleep snoring loudly on the living room floor. Even Gram got a good laugh out of Nikki's antics that day.

Now I was the one adjusting to a new home. It was a difficult time, being away from Princess a little more and rearranging my morning routine to take care of both dogs before leaving for work. It was a crazy schedule, but I loved Princess and Nikki, and they did not seem to mind it as long as they got their fill of attention. The dogs and my work filled the days and nights pretty well. Though I still longed for a family of my own, I had other things to keep me busy and for which to be thankful.

At some point, Nikki started sleeping on the bed with me. She was not allowed under the sheets, but she was allowed on top of the bedspread. I did not mind, especially in the colder months. During the summer months, Nikki preferred to sleep on the floor at the foot of the bed in front of the open windows. Many nights I watched her sleeping while my mind wondered what the future would be like for us.

In the summer of 2003, Nikki chased a lady riding a bicycle on the road. Nikki also followed a guy running down the road late one evening. I dragged her back to the house both times and told her she was not to cross a certain point in the yard. She looked attentive, but did not quite get what I meant. She ran off again, chasing a couple walking on the road one late Saturday afternoon.

Sighing, I said, "Nikki, this is the last straw. You are going to stay in the yard no matter who or what passes by on the road. Do you understand?"

I wanted her to have the freedom to walk around without being tied. There had to be a way to train her without being restrained. After some thought, I decided to use Nikki's favorite activity as a teaching mechanism. Since she loved to play ball, I threw the ball to all the areas of the yard she was allowed. She brought the ball back and waited for me to throw again. We did this through the summer months, and Nikki caught on quickly. She was a very intelligent dog, and I had faith in her that she would succeed. Playing ball lengthened the time required to do my work, but it kept Nikki safe and both of us out of trouble with Gram.

Gram retired from work that summer. She was eighty years old, and health issues were starting to take a toll. Though she missed the social aspect of her work, she happily gave up rising early each day to make the drive to work on time. To fill her free time, Gram sat on the porch with Nikki, watching the cars go by and the wildlife in the surrounding fields. With a fixed income, Gram could not keep the house, so I bought it from her. After all the papers were signed, Gram said, "It's your headache now."

Her tone was half playful, half sincere because the house really needed a lot of repairs at this point. Nikki and I assessed each item on the to-do list and prioritized projects based on resources. We spent many nights and weekends taking measurements, reading how-to books, and researching contractors for some of the bigger projects. This was a new beginning for all of us, and the outcome would play a huge part in our lives.

Chapter Six
Renovations and Reconsiderations

On Thanksgiving Day, Nikki helped me tear apart the indoor porch. Gram was not happy, which was understandable since she wanted to cook in the adjacent kitchen.

"Lisa, why do you have to do that today?" Gram asked.

"Well, I have four days in a row off from work since it is a holiday and I want to use the time to my advantage," I replied.

"Oh, what am I going to do with you? You and your big ideas," Gram said as she shook her head and headed to the kitchen.

Nikki looked at me as if to say: *Well, what do we do now?*

For a moment, I hesitated. My intent was not to upset Gram, but rather to improve the house. Despite my attempts to explain the need for change, Gram did not understand. After a few deep breaths, I went back to removing the old paneling, ceiling tile, and wood trim. Nikki was very good at staying out of the way and at carrying smaller pieces of debris outside to the discard pile. We worked all day gutting the room. Before too late into the night, we started installing insulation board on the outer walls.

The next day after my morning run, we finished the insulation and started putting up new paneling. The paneling took longer because I had to cut the pieces more accurately and make provisions for electrical outlets and switches. Nikki watched intently as I measured and marked the panels before cutting. By Sunday night, we had finished the paneling, installed ceiling tile, and put in new lighting.

The next weekend, we built a cupboard to house linens, dog items, and other supplies. We placed Nikki's crate by the storm door so she could entertain herself and guard the house. I positioned Gram's little table where she sat when putting her hair up in curlers adjacent to the bathroom wall. This table had been next to the wall since my childhood. A large mirror hung on the wall above the table. Gram used this mirror to see better as she rolled her hair into the curlers.

When the project was complete, Gram said, "This is nice. Now I can see better when I put up my hair."

Nikki looked at me as if to say: *I knew she'd come around eventually. You just need to approach things a bit different to get her to buy into your big ideas beforehand instead of after.*

Nikki spent many hours sitting by the storm door in the sun. Often I sat with her, contemplating life. It was Nikki's way of teaching me to relax a bit, and our quiet time together did wonders for my soul. Sometimes we simply sat staring into space, and other times I wrote poetry about what we saw before us or drew sketches of things I wanted to change in the house. Every time was special because it was just Nik and me with God watching over us.

On many nights while Gram sat putting her hair in curlers, Nikki sat with her, watching every move. Gram talked softly, usually with a bobby pin in the corner of her mouth, to Nikki while I looked on from my seat at the kitchen table.

Life was quiet, mostly stable, and full of things to do. Though Gram was able to do less around the house, I enjoyed the extra work. Nikki was always with one of us as we worked. If she grew bored with what we were doing, she entertained herself by watching the birds outside or the cows across the road. Sometimes, she went to take a nap, either in her crate or on her dog bed behind Gram's recliner in the living room.

Chapter Seven
Reasons and Relationships

One day, I decided to invite some friends over for dinner. I made a batch of chocolate chip cookies the day before for us to have for dessert. Not thinking, I put the cookies on a plate, wrapped the plate in plastic wrap, and set the plate on the old hutch Gram had in the corner of the kitchen. When I came home from work the next day, Gram met me at the door with the empty plate, neatly wrapped in the plastic.

"I ran to the store and came back to find the empty plate. I think Nikki ate the cookies," Gram said.

Horrified and scared, I looked at Nikki. Her stomach was puffed out like a balloon. She put her head down low when we made eye contact. Immediately, I had an immense fear because I thought Nikki was going to die from eating all the chocolate chips that were in the cookies. It was too late to call the vet, so I prayed that Nikki would be fine after having a few hours of rest. She appeared somewhat relieved that I did not yell at her. *How could I reprimand her when I was afraid of losing her?*

Then I remembered I had company coming for dinner, but had no dessert to offer them. I used up most of the baking ingredients in the house when I made the cookies. Our guests were due to arrive in an hour. *Oh, how do I get myself into such predicaments?*

Scanning the cupboards for ideas, I found just enough ingredients to make an oatmeal dessert that did not take long to bake. Quickly, I mixed butter, flour, brown sugar, cinnamon, and oats in a bowl. Nikki sat at my feet while I worked. I kept checking on her to make sure she did not show signs of illness. It was not how I had planned to begin the evening, but sometimes our best plans have to surrender to life's events.

I thought I'd be able to get through dinner without anyone knowing what Nikki had done, but Gram decided to tell our guests about the whole ordeal. I wanted to sink through the floor when Gram said, "Nikki ate the first dessert, so Lisa made this instead."

Being new to playing hostess, I felt lost and inadequate to fill the role. Gram's rendition of the story was a little less than accurate, which did not help matters. Our guests were quite amused, but I sat silently watching Nikki and worrying she would get sick.

After our guests left, I took Nikki outside and stared at the stars. Somewhere up there, our future was written and known. Down on earth, we were unaware of the details or the sequence of events leading us to where we needed to be. Although I feared what would happen to Nikki, my faith told me it was out of my hands. All we could do was wait.

Nikki did not get sick, much to my relief. I called the vet the next day to ask about symptoms and precautions. The vet laughed at the story, then explained that since Nikki was rather large, she most likely would be in a little discomfort for a day or so until the cookies passed through her system. The vet's analysis turned out to be correct. Within two days, Nikki was her normal self.

Breathing a huge sigh of relief, I went about my daily routine feeling thankful for the outcome. Days went by amid the humdrum of life for a while, but then things took a turn in a different direction. Nikki was fine, but Princess was not. It was the beginning of a rollercoaster ride through vet visits, prayers, good and bad days, and a lot of inner angst.

In the spring of 2004, Princess was diagnosed with a tumor in her spleen. The prognosis was not good. Nikki and I spent a lot of time with Princess while trying to make the best of the situation. Princess was now thirteen years old. She had been with my family and me since she was three months old. Memories of her as a puppy and growing into canine adulthood flooded my mind. Princess and I spent a lot of time together. Although Nikki was a big dog, filling Princess' paws was not going to be an easy task—or so I thought.

Then it dawned on me that every German shepherd I had owned had his or her own personality. Every one of them taught me lessons in life, faith, hope, and love. Each dog had a unique way of teaching and learning. This uniqueness was part of the fabric of my relationship with them. It was also what made each dog special in his or her own way. Gradually, I reasoned that I should be thankful for what each dog offered, whether large or small, fancy or plain, complex or simple. God made every one of them for a reason. I would come to realize these reasons in time—not in my time—but in God's time.

Chapter Eight

Fate and Furry Friends

Princess' condition and symptoms worsened to the point where she could not function on her own. Conversations with the vet pointed in pretty much one direction, no matter how we viewed the matter. It was a tough decision for me, but one I knew had to be made. She deserved to be in peace, and to be free of pain. On March 10, 2005, Princess was put to sleep. She passed in my arms shortly after 7:30 in the evening. My parents and I buried her in the back yard under the apple tree, which stood guard over all of our beloved canine companions who had passed from this life.

Nikki and I visited Princess' grave in my parents' back yard frequently. Nikki sat next to me while I prayed and cried. Upon returning home, I wrote poetry or stories about my dogs as a way to work though the emotions inside. It was very therapeutic for me, and made me appreciate Nikki even more each day. It also made me realize I wanted another dog—not to fill the void—but rather to fill my desire to live life more fully.

After some searching on the Internet, I found a young, male Black Labrador available at the local dog shelter. I went to see him on December 20, 2005. He was a little distracted at first, which should have been a red flag for me. However, I shrugged it off as shelter behavior. Kneeling down, I called for him to come to me. He ran over, spun around in a tight circle, and leaned into me with a wiggle. His eyes met mine, and I was smitten.

"Can I pick him up tomorrow evening? I need to go get him a crate tonight so he will have his own place to sleep," I explained to the shelter director.

"Yes, tomorrow will be fine," the director replied.

Returning home, I took Nikki upstairs to my bedroom and explained she would soon have a brother who could be her companion. Nikki listened intently, her head cocked to one side with both ears straight up. Her eyes sparkled playfully like many times before, which was her sign of approval to me. I should have told Gram, but thought she might like a surprise, especially since it was so close to Christmas.

The next night, I picked up my new four-legged companion at the shelter. He had been known there as Duke Ellington because he liked to "sing the blues" according to the director. On the way home, I found out he sure could sing, but was way out of tune. As he howled his head off, I calmly told him I wanted to change his name to Luke. He didn't seem to care what I called him, as long as I paid attention to him.

I pulled up the driveway, went into the house to get Nikki, and opened the back of the Jeep so they could meet. Luke looked a little scared when Nikki leaped up next to him. He looked so small next to Nikki's large frame. They sniffed each other without showing any signs of rejection.

Nikki led the way into the house as Luke and I followed. I had Luke on a leash so he would not run ahead and spoil the surprise. We found Gram sitting in her favorite chair in the living room and watching television.

"Hey, Gram! This is Luke. He's going to be staying with us. What do you think?" I asked half full of excitement, half full of fear.

"Lisa! What do we need another dog for? Take him back to wherever you found him," Gram replied.

"But Gram, Christmas is in less than three days. We can't leave him in the shelter for Christmas! He's a bright little fellow, and cute, too! Aw, Gram, please don't be difficult," I said.

"Well, he is cute. But you know I don't like male dogs. They go to the bathroom on everything. Lisa, why do you do these things? You have such big ideas sometimes. Where is he going to sleep?" Gram asked.

"I got him his own crate. We can put it in the kitchen where he'll have easy access to the water dish and the door. He is already house trained. The shelter workers think he is about one-and-a-half years old. Isn't he adorable?" I pleaded.

"Well, alright, but after Christmas, we're going to have to think about this more," Gram said as she turned the volume on the television up higher.

Nikki and Luke sat listening attentively to the entire conversation. They looked up at me as if to ask me to translate for them. Seeing Nikki's sparkling eyes and Luke's boyish grin did me in emotionally. I took them into the kitchen and explained we'd have to convince Gram everything would be fine.

I think Luke may have misinterpreted what I meant by convincing Gram, for he did all the wrong things. Stealing Gram's Kleenex, digging in the garbage can, and becoming an expert thief at sneaking food off the counter did not help his cause. Despite all his faults, Nikki and I could not love him more. She relished the attention he gave to her, and I could not help but be in awe of his dexterity and intelligence.

Luke made Nikki look very good because he was so bad. He ran away on several occasions, and his wandering got him into deep trouble. I had to ground him for life from the freedom of being untied in the yard. He protested by whining, but I could not take the risk of him running along the road or tormenting my uncle's cows in the fence across the road.

"Sorry, buddy, but this is for your own good," I said as I installed a cable for him to use when he was out in the yard. Of course, he found a way to unclip the hook on the cable and to take off in pursuit of whatever struck his fancy. The first time he broke free, Nikki came running to me as if to say: *He's on the loose! You'd better go after him.*

I always thanked Nikki for coming to get me. She seemed to smile in return, giving me a lick on the hand or face. She sure knew how to behave and how to calm my nerves. Luke was the exact opposite of Nikki. He was somewhat of an outlaw or a rebel, always finding trouble without much effort and putting stress into situations that otherwise should have been calm.

Chapter Nine
Life Lessons

Nikki, Luke, and I spent that winter getting acquainted and planning for our next big remodeling adventure—the kitchen. This would be a huge undertaking, so we spent four months planning, staying up until midnight, going over samples, taking dimensions, and designing a new layout. We spent hours studying books on how to do wiring, plumbing, framing, drywall, and different types of flooring. Nikki was content to sit by my chair or at my feet as I studied the books and sketched up ideas, but Luke had no patience for reading. Instead, he found ways to chew my books and spit out the pieces all over the floor.

I tried to include Gram in the planning, asking her what colors she liked, if it would be nice to have the sink moved closer to the window, and if she would like more cupboard space. Quickly, I learned Gram hated change, and she had no interest in cooperating on this project.

"Lisa, you'll never be able to redo this whole kitchen by yourself," Gram challenged.

"Well, Gram, I'm going to try," was my response—and try we did with all our might.

Gram was very upset when Nikki, Luke, and I began demolition on April 1, 2006. We gutted the entire room, all the way down to the studs and floor joists. Nikki and Luke helped by chewing on the debris, taking my tools, and carrying pieces of wood out to the discard pile.

The house was built in the late 1800s. The kitchen had been added on sometime in the early 1900s. The dust and dirt were phenomenal. When I tore out the old tin ceiling, about fifty years worth of walnuts tumbled to the floor. Nikki loved to chew on hard things, so she started chomping away at the walnuts.

"Nik, don't do that! You'll get sick," I said.

She looked at me with that sparkle in her eye. Too tired to argue, I let her do as she wished, while I shoveled walnuts into garbage bags. I vacuumed for two hours straight to rid the room of all the dirt. *What a mess!* That night (or I guess I should say the following morning, since we did not go to bed until after midnight) I prayed that God would help us through the parts of the project that were unknown or new to us.

The dogs and I worked on the kitchen on weekends and in the evening hours during the week. When they got tired, they sat together in the living room on their dog bed. Sometimes Nikki would come nudge me around 10:00 PM as if to say: *I think it is time to stop now and go to bed.*

Gram was difficult at first, but once the insulation, drywall, and subfloor were installed, she softened. While I worked on the kitchen, she called her sisters to give them progress reports.

"Lisa got most of the drywall hung today. Tomorrow, she's going to do start taping the seams. Then she has to prime and paint...Oh, yes, it will be nice when she's done..."

All the research and planning I did really helped, for I was able to keep the appliances in working order throughout the project. The only major inconvenience was doing dishes in the bathroom sink or in the laundry tub down in the basement for a few days. Nikki and Luke inspected my work each day or night, and occasionally moved things around on their own. Luke apparently did not like my drywall work in the one corner, so he ate it. *Leave it to Luke to be picky.*

Nikki seemed to like the new ceramic tile floor as she pranced around it like a queen holding court. Summer was approaching, and she discovered the vent where the cool air from the air conditioner flowed. It became a favorite spot for her, for it was cool in summer, and warm in winter from the furnace's heat.

We finished up in mid June, much to everyone's relief. All those late nights and ten-hour days on weekends took a toll on everyone. I ended up very run down and sick in bed for a few days in early July. Nikki sat on the bed with me the whole time, basking in the fact that my attention was back on her and Luke, instead of on the kitchen. We listened to the stereo or the sounds from outside the bedroom window. Sometimes, she cuddled up next to me like a little child. Her presence comforted me as I wondered about the future. Burying my face in her fur, I realized Nikki smelled like April Fresh Downy.

We spent the remainder of the summer playing ball, mowing grass, doing yard work, and taking lots of walks. Gram sat on the porch with Luke and Nikki to supervise my work. Sometimes she would ask, "Can you get the hose out for me so I can water my flowers?"

Gram could do little chores, but had trouble lifting and moving things, so the hose was an obstacle for her. I uncoiled the hose so Gram could reach all of the flowers. Nikki escorted Gram throughout the process, making sure Gram did not trip on the hose or lose her balance. Watching them made me smile. When they were done, Gram dropped the hose and said, "You can put this away now."

After a brief break from remodeling the house, the dogs and I started renovating the spare room downstairs over Thanksgiving. Gram asked, "Lisa, why do you insist on doing these things on holidays?"

"Well, Gram, holidays are the only occasions when I have large chunks of time off from work. I can get a good deal done without being interrupted," I replied.

She shook her head and sighed. Gram protested all the changes while providing some history on the house. This history explained why I had to remove so many layers of building materials from the walls, ceilings, and floors.

"The house was empty for a while before we bought it. That's how we got it for such a good price. The walls were cracked or covered over with wallpaper that was ugly. Some of your uncles were out of work at the time, so we had them work on different things for us. I didn't want the mess that would come with ripping everything out, so we just went over top with paneling," Gram explained in somewhat of a nostalgic tone.

"That's pretty interesting," I said to Gram as I stared at all the layers, dust, and dirt. None of the walls were even, straight, square, or level. I had to assess each one and decide which corner made the most sense to work off of as a starting point to make things level and square.

Nikki did her best to keep Gram occupied. Luke took all my tools as I worked on the room. Fortunately, it was a small room, so it did not take as long as the kitchen to renovate. The dogs and I finished right before Christmas, took a break for a week, and gutted the living room. Nikki led the clean up crew, picking up debris and nibbling at little pieces of wood. We finished the living room in February. I turned my focus outdoors and started planning a landscaping project for the coming spring months.

Although Gram had thoroughly protested the changes, she sure seemed happy to show off the renovations to her sisters and to other guests. She also spent hours on the phone at night giving detailed descriptions of the rooms to friends. Nikki often sat at Gram's feet or by Gram's chair as the conversations rambled through the hours. Sometimes, Nikki's eyes would lock with mine as Gram was talking. Nikki seemed to be saying: *I told you she'd be fine with the changes once you were done with all the messy parts.*

Chapter Ten
Storms Within

Nikki really liked being outside, no matter the weather. She was with me shoveling snow in the cold winter months, cleaning up sticks in the yard during spring rains, scrubbing porch furniture in the hot summer sun, and raking leaves in the chilly fall evenings. As long as I stopped once in a while to throw the ball for her, she stayed near me. Sometimes she wandered up to the apple tree behind the garage to eat any apples that had fallen to the ground, but mostly she stayed close to me.

Occasionally, she got in the way, and I asked her to please move. When she was feeling frisky, she kept getting in my way until the third or fourth time I asked her to move. It was her way of slowing down the pace and getting me to stop long enough to appreciate the moments more fully. Although her methods were rather subtle, Nikki was a very effective and efficient teacher. She trained me very well on what mattered most in life, and she made me recognize that the little, intangible things are simply priceless.

Our landscaping project went very well, but Nikki and Luke ate about half a yard of mulch apiece. They insisted on moving every bush at least once, sometimes eating the leaves, much to my chagrin. We did not get as far as I had hoped before having to focus on fall leaf clean-up and other events that would alter our lives drastically. Had I known what was to come, I would have spent many more relaxing moments with Nikki and Luke.

In mid-September of 2007, Gram got very sick. Mom took her to the doctor for a check up. The doctor informed Mom he thought Gram may have had a mini stroke. He sent Gram back home with some medicine and orders to rest. We were perplexed that Gram had not been sent directly to the hospital, given her symptoms. We followed all the instructions down to the last detail in an effort to make Gram feel better.

Nikki sat by Gram as Gram dozed in her recliner in the living room. Something about Gram did not seem right to me. I could not put my finger on it, but kept a close watch over her. Later that night, Gram needed help walking to the bathroom. She slept in her recliner instead of her bed, which she did from time to time when she was tired. Nikki and I paced back and forth that night trying to calm our nerves. Something was very wrong, but I did not know what or how to explain it, so I prayed with the hope things would be better soon.

The next morning when I woke Gram, she could not walk at all. I carried her to the bathroom and back to her recliner before I realized what had happened. Looking at Gram's face, I could see one side was twisted in an odd expression. I called my mom right away, "Mom, I need some help. Something is very wrong with Gram. Please hurry!"

We rushed Gram to the hospital shortly after 5:00 AM. A concerned look came over Nikki's face when we carried Gram out of the house. Nikki had every reason to be worried. Gram had had a stroke, and nothing in our lives would ever be the same again.

Gram spent the next week in the hospital and the next month in a rehabilitation center. Nikki missed Gram immensely, and was sick for a few days. It was the first time I knew Gram to be away from the house for an extended period. She worked for years, but always came home for the evening. Life was different. I focused on the dogs more and visited Gram every other night in rehab. Every time I came home, Nikki looked at me eagerly as if she was expecting Gram to appear.

"Oh, Nikki, I'm sorry, but Gram will be away for a few more days. She needs to regain some strength. She can't use her left arm or leg, so we're going to have to help her and be patient. You can do that, can't you, Nik?" I said as I wondered how well we —or should I say I—would all adapt.

Nikki stared back at me with a reassuring look, then went to get her ball. Playing ball was her answer to everything. I couldn't blame her. My answer to everything was running or biking, which I did a lot of in the days since Gram got sick. Something about the physical motion and being outside had a calming effect, offering hope despite the apparent mountain that suddenly stood before us.

On October 17, 2007, Gram came back home from rehabilitation. The months that followed were challenging for everyone. The stroke left Gram unable to swallow or talk as she had before. She could not walk without much assistance, could not dress herself, and was miserable but determined to overcome the situation. We did therapy every morning and night. I cooked, cleaned, maintained the yard and vehicles, and tried my best to not get depressed. Mom helped me rearrange the living room, placing the spare bed from upstairs in one corner so Gram could sleep on the first floor of the house. This arrangement made it easier for me to transfer Gram from her wheelchair into bed. It was a struggle, but with Nikki by my side, I knew things would work out eventually.

Each morning, Mom came over before work to help me get Gram ready for the day. I lifted Gram from her bed, transferred her to her wheel chair, and wheeled her to the bathroom while Mom ran hot water and got towels ready. We quickly learned how important timing was in getting Gram washed, dressed, and fed. At one point, my mom said, "This is like the race teams getting the cars ready in the pits."

From that day forward, we called our morning routine NASCAR Gram. On most days, it was a race to make sure everything got done on time so Mom and I could make it to work. We found an adult daycare program Gram could attend three days a week. We really had to have our timing down on those days because a van came at a scheduled time to pick Gram up and take her to the daycare center. On days when Gram could not attend daycare, my one aunt came to stay with Gram, Nikki, and Luke so my mom and I could go to work. On these days, we did not have to hurry as much, but still had to have things in order so Gram was ready before my aunt arrived.

In the evenings, we did NASCAR Gram in reverse, though we usually did not have to be as quick. Nikki and Luke soon learned the difference between the morning and evening routines, and how these routines affected them. Nikki often sat to the side to supervise, but Luke insisted in crawling under Gram's wheel chair to play a part in the activities. He also developed very adept skill at sneaking Gram's Kleenex from her pajama pocket, which always resulted in Gram yelling, "LUKE! NO!"

We only had one bathroom in the house. It was difficult to get Gram in and out of the bathroom with her wheel chair, so I gutted the bathroom and installed a seated shower and safety bars for Gram. Of course, with the house being so old, there was no insulation, and the plumbing needed redone, which lengthened the time it took to finish the job.

Gram got very sick with an infection and ended up in the hospital before I could finish the bathroom. She came back home, got sick again, and was admitted to the hospital right before Christmas. The doctors said it did not look good. I spent New Year's Eve putting up the last trim pieces in the bathroom. As I worked, I worried Gram would not live to see the bathroom completed. I prayed that Gram would beat the odds and be back home soon. Nikki was by my side the whole time. Luke provided some comic relief by stealing my hammer. It was a very long, late night for us.

When we finally did go to sleep, I buried my head in Nikki's body, breathing in her April Fresh Downy smell as I cried. I simply did not know how to handle what I felt inside. Nikki gave me a serious, but caring look. Her eyes watered a bit, sparkling in the dim rays of the night light. Nikki and Luke cuddled next to me on the bed as I prayed to God to give us the strength to deal with whatever was to come.

Gram managed to make it back home for a few weeks in January. She had all kinds of therapists, nurses, and social workers visiting her. My mom, sister, and I used up all our vacation time trying to care for Gram. When my aunt learned of our dilemma, she offered to stay with Gram and let in any of Gram's attendants.

Nikki did not like this situation at all. Our home was being invaded by strangers all hours of the day. Mom, my sister, and I were worn out and starting to get run down. Things were not good. Every night, the dogs went upstairs to bed with me, and I buried my head under the covers to cry. Sensing my uneasiness, Nikki placed her paw on my leg or arm as if to say all would be made well. Although I knew she was right, I did not know what kind of time frame we had to deal with the many issues arising each day.

The breaking point came on February 6, 2008. Gram got sick and had to be admitted to the hospital due to another infection. My mom called a family meeting to discuss options. We were all worn out, and we all agreed that Gram needed more care than we could give her. The doctors released Gram with the condition she be placed in a nursing care facility where she had access to professional care twenty-four hours a day.

Nikki took Gram's absence at the house very hard. She had grown close to Gram over the years, despite Gram's initial reluctance to accept Nikki's presence in the house. The two of them had formed a bond— not like the one I had with Nikki—but somewhat similar. Nikki was a good sport about the matter as time passed. Gram had more difficulty accepting the situation and moving forward.

Mom and I took turns visiting Gram every other night at the care facility. As soon as I entered her room each night, Gram asked, "How are my dogs? How is Nikki? Do they miss me? Can I go home with you?"

Our conversation almost always centered on the dogs, which was a good distraction for Gram. Mom and I often brought Gram home for weekend visits so she could see the house, the neighborhood, Nikki, and Luke. When the weather was nice, Gram sat on the porch in her wheel chair. Nikki sat on one side of Gram, and Luke sat on the other side. In the colder months, I sat Gram at the kitchen table so she could read the newspaper or look at magazines while I made dinner or did house work. My aunt often came to visit and to eat dinner with us. Afterward, Gram and my aunt talked while I cleaned up the kitchen. Taking Gram back late Sunday afternoon was depressing for everyone, especially Nikki. However, we did the best we could and left the rest to God.

Chapter Eleven

Family Formations

Before Gram had the stroke, I realized my dreams of having a family of my own would not be coming true. As a girl, I always wanted three children, preferably a boy and two girls. For some reason, I liked the name Nancy Jean and wanted that name for my youngest child. Why I wanted it to be this way, I have no idea, but the dream stuck with me.

After coming to terms with being a single adult, I figured it was time to accept the fact I was not going to have children of my own. I told myself that I would have my dogs instead to love. Since Nikki kind of sounds like Nancy, I decided to give her Jean as a middle name. Jean is my mom's middle name, which is why I wanted to pass it on through the family. Luke became Luke James, after my Uncle Jim and the fact he was an outlaw like Jesse James, always misbehaving despite Nikki's attempts to help me correct him.

Nikki Jean and Luke James filled the role of children in my family fantasy and in real life (and to some extent, so did Gram). We were quite dysfunctional, but we loved each other, and that is all that mattered to us. I finally found fruition to my dreams and hope for a brighter future. Overwhelmed with emotion after waiting for so long to see a ray of light, I wrote poems for each dog. Nikki's went like this:

Nikki Jean

When I was young I dreamed
Of having a little girl named Nancy Jean.
She would be the light of my life
Running in the yard outside
Golden curls bouncing in the wind
Yelling, "Mom, chase me again!"
Life would alter my plans
For reasons I now understand
And instead of a daughter of my own
I would give a home
To a German shepherd I would come to meet
Named Nikki Jean.

Oh, Nikki Jean
You came to me
From heaven I swear.
You made me aware
Of what matters most in life
And I find
Myself thanking God every day
For sending you to me
Nikki Jean.

Now in the ways I see
You Nikki Jean
As a light in my life
Running in the yard outside
Ears bouncing in the wind
As you chase the ball again.
Life sure has altered my plans
For reasons I now understand.
You are as close
As a daughter of my own
Giving love unconditionally,
You are my Nikki Jean.

The dogs and I kept busy around the house in the spring and summer of 2008. I declared it the year of the dig. We dug drainage ditches around the house foundation to alleviate issues with water entering the basement, planted twenty-three trees on the property, created mulch areas in the yard, and dug an indoor French drain in the cellar. Late that summer, Nikki helped me build a small stone wall around the old hand pump in the yard. The wall bordered the driveway and curved around the pump slab. Next to the pump slab, I built a sidewalk and a ramp for Gram so she could enter the house with her wheelchair.

Nikki and I took stones from the old barn foundation on the property to build the wall. Of course, we had to play ball after placing a stone or two, so the project took quite a while to complete even though the wall itself was less than two feet high and thirty-six feet long. Nikki dropped her ball by the next stone she wanted me to place. I threw her ball, hurried up to place the stone, and turned around to find her back by my side waiting for her ball to be thrown again. The wall took about a week's worth of evenings to complete, but it turned out well.

In November, I got a call from a former coworker. Someone she knew had gotten a German shepherd puppy and could not keep it. She wanted to know if I was interested in adopting this puppy. I kindly explained that with Gram's situation, I felt it was not a good time to do so. However, I agreed to look at the dog and to ask others I knew if they could help with finding a home.

Well, within two minutes of meeting Sadie, she was sitting next to me, carefully watching my every move and assessing my skills as a dog owner. She was black and tan, thin as can be, and full of life and energy. Her eyes met mine, pleading: *Please take me home with you. I'll be a good dog, but I need out of my current situation and a little understanding to help me grow.*

I could not say no, so I put Sadie in the back of my Jeep and drove home. As I drove, I wondered how I managed to get myself into these situations in life. Silently, I prayed that Nikki and Luke would be alright with a playmate, at least for a while. I really did not think this was a good idea, but it was obvious Sadie needed help. Being a dog lover, I felt obligated to get her out of a bad situation.

Oddly, my biggest concern was Nikki. She had accepted Luke quite well, but another female dog in the house might not work for her. At this point in life, we did not need any more issues, and I had not fully recognized how God works in mysterious ways to help us with our needs. Pulling into the driveway, I braced myself for the dogs' first encounter.

In my mind, the best plan was to introduce Nikki to Sadie first. I let Nikki out of the house and walked to the Jeep to get Sadie. Nikki stood on the porch waiting patiently. I think she may have thought I was bringing Gram home for a visit, which is why she opted to stay on the porch and not approach the Jeep. Nikki had learned that getting Gram in and out of the Jeep was a process. The best way for her to help was to wait until I rolled Gram in her wheel chair along the sidewalk and up the ramp onto the porch.

Upon seeing Nikki, Sadie barked a few times, tail wagging, eyes bright with excitement. Sadie walked right up to Nikki and licked her nose. Nikki circled a few times before acting as if she had found a long-lost friend. I breathed a huge sigh of relief and took a deep breath before introducing Sadie to Luke. Luke immediately took to Sadie, for she gave him her full attention, which is what he wanted most from everybody.

All went well, but I was nervous because I had my cousin coming to the house for a visit in less than two hours. Why I do these kinds of things with so much going on in my life is beyond me. My cousin was very accepting of the situation. We had a nice talk while watching the three dogs get acquainted that night.

Sitting on the couch, my cousin remarked, "She is cute, Lisa, and so bright-eyed."

I looked at Sadie sitting quietly in a dog crate I had borrowed from my mom. Sadie's huge ears stood straight up like satellites above her small body. She listened to every word we spoke and watched intently, studying our movements and gestures. My heart was already won over by Sadie, but my mind kept protesting the logistics and real life aspects of the matter.

After my cousin left, I did a lot of thinking and praying about Sadie. She needed a home and was absolutely adorable. I kept asking Nikki and Luke if they thought we could handle a different routine for a while until Sadie was house trained. Luke seemed not to care either way. He knew his place in our family, and he was happy no matter what life brought our way.

Nikki was more mature and seemed to contemplate the situation deeply before giving me a look that said: *I know you well enough to know you are too compassionate at times and that you often get us in over our heads. However, I also know we have learned to adapt together and we are too determined not to accept the challenge of helping Sadie by giving her a home. I'll support you in your decision either way.*

The timing was all wrong, but when in life is timing right? Questions filled my mind as I tried to get some rest. It was a fitful night with me considering each aspect of the situation. I prayed to God for guidance. By morning, knew what I had to do for all of us.

The next day, I gave Sadie her middle name. She would be Sadie Jane. My cousin's middle name is Jane, and since she was Sadie's first visitor, I thought it was fitting. After thirty-four years of dreaming about it, I finally had my three kids—but not in a traditional sense. Nikki and Sadie played well together. Luke enjoyed the extra attention Sadie gave him. Although I felt overwhelmed at times, I had to admit Sadie added an element to our lives that made us feel more complete.

Gram came home for a visit the next weekend. She gave me an earful about having another dog. It was the Nikki speech all over again, only worse. I just let her talk as I held Sadie in my arms. At this point, all I wanted was to get through life somewhat intact and to find some inner peace. The dogs were helping accomplish this task. It was rough at times, trying to be there for everyone's needs, but everything happens for a reason. I knew God had sent Sadie to us for a reason. What that reason was became clear sooner than I expected—and in a life-altering way.

Chapter Twelve
Finding Friends

The dogs and I managed to get through the cold winter months pretty well. Sadie had to sleep on the floor by the bed because there was not enough room for all three dogs and me in my single bed. I bought her a dog bed and put it next to my bed so she would not feel left out. On a few very cold nights, Sadie ended up on top of me or Nikki in my bed. This resulted in some huge fits of laughter in the morning when all of us woke up with our bodies twisted into strange configurations in an effort to not fall off of the bed.

When the nights were not as chilly, Nikki moved to the dog bed with Sadie. Nikki always loved her dog beds, but Luke ate most of them—nineteen to be exact— after the first week. I prayed that Luke would break his bad habit and not chew Sadie's dog bed. Nikki and Sadie slept together until about 2:00 AM when Sadie had to go out. Sometimes after going out, Sadie crawled on top of the bed with me until we got up at 4:00 AM.

Upon rising, I let the dogs out, brushed them, fed them, and did my morning exercises before getting ready for work. Before leaving the house, I let the dogs out again, made sure they had enough water, and gave each dog a hug. My days were usually a blur with so much going on at my job. At lunch time, things slowed down a bit because I walked with several friends. We talked as we walked, often erupting in laughter at stories about their families or my adventures with Nikki, Luke, and Sadie.

I was always the first person in the office at work, so I had the duties of turning on lights, making copies, and preparing information for my coworkers before they arrived. One morning before Christmas, I turned on the lights, walked to my desk, and stared in amazement. On and under the desk were presents galore, including a dog crate, a huge bag of dog food, a collar with a name tag for Sadie, dog treats, and a card. The card was signed Your Secret Santa in handwriting that I recognized, but could not remember where I had seen before.

Somewhat perplexed, I carted all the gifts to my Jeep because I needed room to work. A coworker arrived some time later. I asked him if he knew anything about the gifts. All he would say was, "The ladies sure had fun bringing all that stuff up here after you left yesterday."

I started putting the clues together and determined my Secret Santa was really my walking friends. Later in the morning, I confronted the woman whom I suspected was the ring leader, "You wouldn't happen to know anything about a Secret Santa, would you?"

The look on her face gave her away. I said, "You're busted. Who else was in on it?"

She led me into the office where two other friends worked. We all laughed and cried. I asked, "Why did you do all that for us?"

They explained they had noticed I was concerned about the holidays coming and they thought I might be worried about having enough resources to give the dogs a nice Christmas. Through our walking talks, they had learned of the many expenses I had with Gram's care and with adding Sadie to the family. It was their way of helping a friend in need.

I thanked them for their kindness and concern and went back to my desk. The coworker I had talked with earlier noticed the lost look on my face. He asked me if something was wrong.

"No, I just don't know why they did all that," I replied.

"Lisa, sometimes it still pays to be a nice guy, or in your case, gal. You do a lot for people around here, and the ladies just wanted to let you know they appreciate all you do," my coworker explained.

When I arrived home that night, I let the dogs out and fed them. They all looked so happy: Nikki with her eyes sparkling, Luke with his boyish grin, and Sadie with her huge ears on her tiny puppy body. As I carried all the gifts into the house, I said, "Kids, we just hit the friendship and Christmas lottery!"

God sure knows how to provide when we need it most. It was the best Christmas I ever had, and one of the best lessons in life I ever experienced. It also made future events easier to handle despite the conditions.

Chapter Thirteen
Forks in the Road

We started what I called Phase III of our landscaping project in the spring of 2009. Nikki helped me mulch, plant bulbs, and dig two new mulch beds in the yard. Of course, we had to play ball while doing these things. We also planted ten more trees and moved around some bushes. Luke and Sadie supervised from their tie-outs by the porch and the garage.

Gram continued to come for visits on weekends. I picked her up early Saturday morning. The dogs sat with her while I worked around the house. We talked and played cards when Gram felt like doing so. I made dinner for everyone and cleaned up afterward. My mom took Gram back to the care facility Sunday night. We also did this on holidays when Mom and I had time off from work to attend to all of Gram's needs.

Life was moving along somewhat normally until I noticed Nikki having some trouble with her back legs. Once she got up and moved around a bit, she was fine. After sleeping at night or long periods lying on the floor, she sometimes had difficulty moving around. She was deemed healthy by the vet her annual checkup in April, so I was kind of confused by this behavior in the middle of June. I called the vet to make another appointment.

On Thursday, June 25, 2009, the vet felt Nikki's spine and found an area that seemed to be abnormal. Dr. Ann said that Nikki had an inflammation of sorts that was causing pain in the spine. This pain made it difficult for Nikki to move her back legs. After talking things through, we agreed to try some anti-inflammatory medication and antibiotics—Nikki had a slight fever—for a few days to see if the symptoms subsided.

Nikki responded well to the medication. She seemed to be her old self by Saturday. Late Sunday afternoon, Nikki began breathing rather oddly. After a few minutes, she was fine, but drank a lot of water. I was concerned and decided to call Tim and Mary, Nikki's former owners. After all, I had promised to keep them informed. They had kept in touch and visited Nikki on several occasions, so I felt they would want to know. They were not home, so I left a message for them.

Monday morning, I called the vet to make an appointment for Nikki to have blood work and x-rays taken on Thursday. Nikki was acting normally, but something inside me said something was wrong inside of her. I prayed I was wrong.

Tim called me back Tuesday evening and agreed to come see Nikki. He wanted to wait until after her vet appointment on Thursday to set up a day and time to visit. I agreed we would know more after Nikki's appointment, and said I would call if anything changed.

Nikki's medicine made her need to go out more often, so I came home at lunch time to let the dogs out. On Thursday, July 2, shortly after noon, I found Nikki in the middle of the kitchen floor breathing very heavily. Immediately, I felt sick inside.

Rushing to her side and kneeling down, I whispered, "Hang on, Nik!"

Nikki's vet appointment was not until 5:45 PM. She needed assistance now, and I had left work thinking I was returning for the afternoon. I knew what had to be done, but I was not sure I had time to do it all. Leaping to the phone, I called the vet and got clearance to bring Nikki into the office as soon as I could get her there. From past experience, I knew time was not on our side, and that every moment was critical.

Nikki always had a stoic aura to her, but for the first time ever, her eyes told me she needed help. Though I tried to stay calm, I felt myself losing the battle. The rock I had leaned upon was giving way to life's changes. I had to switch roles and allow her to lean on me, but I had to find strength in a hurry to do an adequate job.

Within twenty minutes, I was carrying Nikki out to the Jeep. I had to be careful and move with grace so as not to cause her any more issues. She was very still and quiet, not like herself at all. Within another fifteen minutes, we were in Dr. Ann's office. Dr. Ann examined Nikki, talked to me a bit about symptoms and the order of events, and took x-rays and blood samples.

I had to wait outside in the lobby area for the x-rays to be done. With each passing minute, more fear built up inside me. I had been through similar scenarios with four other dogs. History was not in Nikki's or my favor. I prayed my suspicions were wrong, but experience told me my analysis of the situation was right. Reeling with emotion, I felt myself becoming sick.

I had been using Dr. Ann and her husband Ken as veterinarians since Princess was a puppy. They and their staff knew me well by now, and the receptionist noticed my unease.

"It will be okay, Lisa. I know the waiting is hard. Is there something you would like to talk about to pass the time?" she asked.

"It's just hard. Nikki is a very special dog. I did not know her as a puppy, yet we've grown so close in the seven years we've been together. She is now eleven-and-a-half years old. I understand shepherds don't have the longest life expectancy, but I'm not sure I am ready to let go yet..."

Dr. Ann opened the door and called me in the exam room. It was shortly after 2:00 PM. She explained the findings and showed me the x-rays. Nikki had two vertebrae that were abnormal in shape, which were placing pressure in her back and causing the issues with her walking. She had what appeared to be either a small mass or scar tissue on her one lung. The biggest concern was her spleen. It was full of blood. Dr. Ann did a tap to verify the x-ray and showed me a syringe full of blood taken from Nikki's spleen.

The options were exploratory surgery or ultrasound to try to pinpoint the problem, but neither were a guarantee to any type of correction or solution. The other option was to rid Nikki of the pain and put her to sleep.

My head started to spin as I choked back tears. "Can I go outside for some fresh air for a moment?" I asked.

"Sure. Take your time. Nikki is resting comfortably now with the help of some medicine. I understand this is hard, and I'm sorry, Lisa," Dr. Ann replied.

Stepping outside the office, I knew in my heart and mind what I had to do. My only problem was it hurt tremendously, and I did not have much time. It was a holiday weekend—the Fourth of July was Saturday. This was not how I had envisioned spending the holiday. It was also Sadie's first birthday. Suddenly, I felt very ill, but Nikki's condition was more serious than mine, and I needed to act quickly, despite how I felt.

I called my mom, explained the situation to her, and told her what I felt I should do. She agreed to my plan and said she would try to help me as soon as she got home from work that night. Then I called my sister. I needed Tim and Mary's phone number, but did not have it in my cell phone. My sister agreed to go get the phone number from Gram's old address book at home.

I went back into the office to sit with Nikki in the recovery kennel area. My sister called back shortly after I sat down on the floor next to Nikki.

"Lisa, is there anything else you need?" my sister asked.

After a long moment, I answered, "No, just pray we have enough time to do what we need to do."

Looking at Nikki, I called Tim and Mary. I had to leave a message. Nikki and I sat together for a few minutes. I stroked her fur and tried to think of something to say to her. She looked at me with a bit of a glimmer in her eye. It was obvious the medicine was working because she was breathing normally.

My cell phone rang, startling me for a moment. The voice on the other end was Mary's. "Lisa, I got your message. How is Nikki now?" she asked.

Struggling with words, I explained the situation. Mary said she would get in touch with Tim. I told her I would call her back shortly, after I had talked to Dr. Ann again.

After about fifteen minutes, I mustered up enough strength to rise from my spot on the floor next to Nikki. I walked into the office area to inform Dr. Ann of my decision. Dr. Ann agreed to come to my house after her office hours to put Nikki to sleep. She sent

Nikki and me home with an IV full of pain medication to keep Nikki somewhat comfortable for the next five hours. Our only fear was Nikki being able to hold on that long. She had perked up with the IV in her, so we felt we had a good chance of making it.

Chapter Fourteen
Reflections and Rainbows

As soon as we got home, I settled Nikki into a comfortable position in the kitchen. I sat with her, Luke, and Sadie on the floor. In the calmest voice I could muster, I explained to them what was going to happen, "Nikki is very sick. We are going to have to let God take care of her for a while, which means she'll be watching over us, but we won't be able to see her..."

We prayed together, Sadie and Luke huddled around Nikki and me. I cried, burying my head in Luke's neck as he tried to lick up my tears. Sadie looked concerned. Though she was little, she knew Nikki and me well enough to know something major was wrong. Nikki had taught Sadie very well in the short time they had together.

There was still a lot to do, so I had to keep moving. I took Luke and Sadie outside and propped the storm doors open in case Nikki got up enough strength to venture outside. She did not want the IV in her right away, so we postponed doing that for an hour or so.

Taking the digging tools out of the garage, I headed to the apple tree in the side yard. It was Nikki's favorite tree. Just a night earlier, I was out in the yard working and suddenly realized she was not next to me. I found her lying under the tree eating green apples.

The day was rainy, and the ground was easy to dig. However, I hit tree roots below the top soil. Nothing in life like this is ever easy, so I told myself that this too shall pass and what does not kill you makes you stronger. I dug for about ten minutes, went to check on Nikki, beat at the tree roots, went back to check on Nikki, and dug some more.

As I repeated this pattern over and over, I found myself praying to Princess, asking her to show Nikki around once she got to heaven. I also prayed to my Great Aunt Theresa, who had passed away in December, right before Christmas. Aunt Theresa liked Nikki and used to talk to the dogs when she came to visit us. I figured she would not mind helping Nikki find her way to the right place.

Mom rumbled up the driveway in her Jeep as I was digging. We talked briefly, and she left to go visit Gram. We agreed not to tell Gram about Nikki until the weekend. Gram was staying overnight for the Fourth of July holiday, so it would be easier to explain once she arrived. Mom said she would be back as soon as possible.

After about an hour, I had what I considered a nice resting place hewed out of the ground. I was filthy dirty, covered in tears and mud, and very drained.

There was still a lot to do. I cleaned myself up a bit, got the house in order, and moved Nikki to the living room. Once I got her on her bed, I put in the IV, got Luke and Sadie back in the house and into their crates, and tried to prepare for what was going to happen.

Sitting on the floor with Nikki, I went through our life together in my mind and prayed. She was getting weaker. Her breathing was slow but steady. My dad knocked on the door before coming into the house to sit with Nikki and me. Sadie and Luke were abnormally quiet as they peered around the corners of their crates with all eyes on Nikki.

Mary arrived sometime between 5:30 and 6:00 PM. She sat on the floor with Nikki and me, telling stories about when Nikki was a puppy. According to Mary, Nikki was a very gentile dog for how big she was. I recalled Tim describing Nikki as a huge marshmallow the day I adopted her.

"When we went to pick Nikki out of the litter, I felt she was the most beautiful creature I had ever seen," Mary said.

Nikki was happy to see Mary, and appeared even happier when Tim arrived around 7:30 PM. Mom came back around that time as well. So there we sat, talking about life and telling stories about Nikki and the many lessons she had taught us.

Even at eleven-and-a-half years old with time running out, Nikki appeared to be her graceful self. She had the perfect German shepherd face and body. Her eyes still sparkled, though not as bright as when we first met. Leaning down to give her a hug, I caught the faint scent of April Fresh Downy. Her coat was smooth and soft from getting a bath the week before. Sitting next to her was comforting, despite the situation. She always could calm me down better than anyone or anything else in the whole world.

Dr. Ann arrived around 8:00 PM. We said our final goodbyes to Nikki as Dr. Ann got the injection ready.

Holding Nikki in my arms, I whispered, "I love you very much, Nik."

Dr. Ann listened to Nikki's heart through a stethoscope. After a moment, Dr. Ann said, "Her heart has stopped beating. She has passed."

Dr. Ann helped me carry Nikki to the resting spot I had dug earlier. We wrapped Nikki in a soft blanket and placed her in the dirt carefully. I put Nikki's favorite ball, now all chewed up and out of round, on the ground next to her head. We each prayed silently.

Finally, Tim spoke, "Thank you for including us. That was really special."

Dr. Ann gave me a hug and said to call the office if we needed anything. She backed out of the driveway, followed by Tim and Mary. Dad helped me put the dirt back in the hole, and Mom helped me clean up the tools.

After my parents left, I went in the house to get Sadie and Luke. I felt very empty and lost, full of grief, and did not want to sit still. We stayed outside until well after dark that night. I washed and vacuumed the Jeep with tears running down my face and a pit in my stomach. The only thought that filled my mind was: *Oh, Nikki, I miss you so much!*

The sky was cloudy and gray, matching how I felt inside. Darkness seemed to surround me on all sides. Emotions flowed from within like waves in the sea. I found myself staring at the ground for a long time. Out of the corner of my eye, something in the sky caught my attention. Looking up, I saw the clouds had parted, revealing a sky all the colors of the rainbow.

My heart leaped into my throat, for I knew it was a sign that Nikki had made it to heaven, running all the way. Tears streamed down my face. I gathered Luke and Sadie in my arms, and we watched the sky until all the colors faded into the night.

After we went in the house and I had cried until the tears would no longer come, I wrote the following for Nikki:

The Rainbow in the Sky

She was a shining light
In everyone's life,
A faithful companion and loving friend,
Even until the last moment and final breath,
Offering joy and hope
Through the unknown,
Love and faith
On the darkest days,
And strength and security
In the greatest hours of need.
Now she has crossed the divide
To the rainbow in the sky
And is resting in ultimate peace
Waiting for me.

She wore a stoic face
Through the deepest pain,
Offered the best comfort
Through the severest storms,
Taught others how to live again
After being severely broken,

And showed me the way
To brighter days.
Now she has crossed the divide
To the rainbow in the sky
And is resting in ultimate peace
Waiting for me.

Thankful am I
To have had her in my life,
Blessed is my soul
To have had her to hold,
Saddened is my heart
Now that we are apart,
But hopeful am I to someday cross the divide
To the rainbow in the sky
And rest in peace
With her eternally.

Chapter Fifteen

Heartbreaks and Happenstance

The next day was Friday. I woke up with Luke and Sadie on top of me in bed. I felt like the Grand Canyon had been hewed out of me over night. A gentle rain fell upon me during a long run. I wondered if the rain was God's way of helping wash away my sadness and grief.

We stayed busy that day by running errands, cleaning the house, doing laundry, picking berries for jelly, and making a memorial garden under the apple tree for Nikki. I transplanted salvia from behind the garage to Nikki's grave. Nikki helped me plant the salvia two years earlier. The salvia was not growing, and I wondered why until I caught Nikki tearing the flowers off of it. The plant bloomed for the first time the day before Nikki passed. I felt it was only right to place the salvia as the focal point of her garden.

Taking some stones from the old barn foundation, I placed them between other bushes I had planted for Nikki. Doing so reminded me of the wall we built, which brought tears to my eyes. I took Nikki's old porcelain dish from the house, filled it with all the kinds of flowers she had eaten over the years, and placed the dish next to the base of the apple tree. After saying some prayers, I went to spend some time with Luke and Sadie.

Mom went to pick Gram up on Saturday while I went for a long run. I needed space to clear my head so I could explain to Gram what happened with Nikki. I also needed to talk with God because my emotions were taking me on a rollercoaster ride. Returning home all sweaty and teary-eyed, I took a shower and did my best to compose myself while Luke and Sadie watched me carefully.

After helping Gram into her wheel chair and pushing her up to the porch, Gram asked, "Where's Nikki?"

Kneeling down in front of Gram, I told her what happened, "Gram, Nikki got really sick, and I had to take her to the vet. When the vet examined her, she found a mass on Nikki's lung and blood in Nikki's spleen. I'm sorry Gram, but Nikki had to be put to sleep…"

Gram patted my shoulder as I lowered my head and started crying.

"Oh, Lisa! You mean she's in heaven?" Gram asked.

"Yes," I replied.

"Well, I guess it's a good thing you got Sadie when you did. At least Nikki got to show her around the yard and helped you train her...," Gram's voice trailed off.

Gram took the news better than I thought she would, although she did ask a lot of questions about how the events unfolded. Each time she asked, I tried to keep my composure, but it was difficult. The rest of Gram's visit with us was uneventful, save for Luke stealing Gram's Kleenex.

Luke and Sadie were kind of sad, moping around the house with me. The house suddenly seemed too quiet without Nikki clicking her nails on the kitchen floor and barking out the door at the cows across the road. I reasoned life without her was going to be very, very different, and it would take some time to get adjusted.

No matter how much I ran or how busy I kept myself, I could not lose the empty feeling inside. Sadness enveloped me all hours of the day. I knew I had to get out of this funk, but did not know how, so I went to talk to the priest at my church.

Upon hearing my story, the priest said, "Well, you do know dog is God spelled backwards for a reason."

Reflecting upon his words, I did my best to move on with life. Some days were good, others not so much. Nikki had definitely taken a part of me with her, but she also left a part of herself in my heart. Although she was no longer physically present, I sensed her spirit was still with us, and this spirit was with us for a reason. That reason did not remain unknown very long.

Seeing Gram go through the aftereffects of a stroke and losing Nikki rather unexpectedly made me realize life was short. We should be thankful for our blessings, for they can be taken away at any time. With these thoughts in mind, I decided to return to college to finish a bachelor's degree that had been put on hold for a number of reasons.

Going back to school was not easy given my need to work and my other responsibilities, like caring for Luke and Sadie. However, I did the best I could and learned to pray first instead of last in certain situations. I also wrote a lot of poetry and decided to publish a collection of these writings in book form. This was a large undertaking, but I remembered the many times Nikki and I forged ahead through the unknown, and how Nikki's spirit gave me strength.

Each day, I walked Luke and Sadie past Nikki's garden, searching for whatever solutions were necessary to meet life's demands. Sometimes we were short on resources, and I had to make some sacrifices. Then there were times when I lacked understanding and patience, which troubled me. Often, I prayed to both God and Nikki, asking for guidance. My faith told me neither of them would let me down, and time showed me my faith was right.

Although school, work, and regular visits to see Gram at the care facility made for a hectic schedule with few days off, the dogs and I managed to settle into a routine. Of course, there were days when few things went right and frustration hovered over me like a cloud. In these times, I stood by Nikki's grave thinking: *Oh, Nikki. I miss you. What am I going to do?*

Luke and Sadie soon discovered they could be very mischievous without Nikki or Gram to watch over them. Their curiosity got them into a lot of trouble and emptied my bank account quicker than I could put money into it.

One night after a particularly difficult day, I awoke to a crunching sound. Turning on the light, I found Luke eating my eye glasses.

"Luke! No!" I moaned. He kept chomping away at the frame, leaving teeth marks deep into the lenses. There was no way I could see out of them now. Fortunately, I had an old pair that I could use until the eye doctor was able to replace the broken pair.

Walking up to Nikki's grave the next day, I thought: *Oh, Nikki, what am I going to do with Luke and Sadie? They get into the oddest predicaments.*

Not long after the glasses incident, Luke and Sadie took money I had set aside for groceries from the kitchen counter and chewed it into tiny pieces. Out of $107, they left $20 intact.

"Oh, you two! Now what am I going to buy groceries with this week? I don't get paid for another two weeks, and we have other bills to pay," I said with a deep sigh as I started picking up fragments of money from the kitchen and entry floors.

Now I was both upset and worried. Not knowing what to do, I was very quiet all evening. Luke and Sadie sensed my frustration when I did not invite them up on the bed that night. I was beyond tired, slowly sinking into despair from not seeing any break in the array of mishaps in life. Exhausted, I cried myself to sleep and prayed that somehow all would be made right.

The next morning was a test day for me. I should have reviewed the material, but instead painstakingly taped together the money pieces before heading to the bank to see what could be done. Before leaving the house, I told Luke and Sadie, "You guys better pray we can at least get some of this money back. If not, we're in deep, and you two may need to go get jobs."

When I told the ladies at the bank what had happened, they erupted in laughter. Once everyone regained composure, they looked at the money pieces and determined enough was salvaged to verify the cash value. Relieved, I walked out of the bank with replacement money, which allowed me to buy groceries on the way home from class.

Entering the house, Luke and Sadie greeted me calmly and with a bit of hesitation. "It's okay. You did a good job of praying because we got the money back," I said as I put grocery bags on the table.

We had other incidents as well that first year after Nikki passed, including two more eyeglass eating stints and an eaten cell phone. After each incident, I walked to Nikki's grave not knowing what else to do. I felt so lost. Nikki had such a way with Luke and Sadie, always knowing how to correct them and keep them out of trouble. Although I tried, I could not find that magic touch like Nikki. Maybe I needed to spend more time with Luke and Sadie. After all, Nikki and I spent a lot of time together over the years. That time made a huge difference in life. It was worth a try.

So, Luke, Sadie, and I started small with five or ten minutes of what we called quality time. We worked on commands, went for walks, listened to music, and occasionally just sat staring at each other. Things did not change immediately, but after a few months, I saw progress.

I also started playing ball with the dogs. Sadie was fine in the yard and could be left loose, so this was a great way to teach her the property boundaries. At first, I was not sure if she would know what to do, so we walked through it once. The next time I threw the ball, she instantly returned, raring to go for another sprint after the ball. Her stance and mannerisms were similar to Nikki's. Overcome with emotion, I hugged Sadie and cried.

Luke was a bit harder to play with since he could not be trusted loose in the yard. I had to get a little creative with ways to bounce or roll the ball so he could still chase it and not choke himself on his tie out cable. He enjoyed when I bounced the ball on the sidewalk and could jump up to catch it.

Another activity the dogs enjoyed was watching me learn to play guitar. They sat and listened intently as I strummed or picked at the strings. Occasionally, they fell asleep as I played, especially in the late evening hours.

Despite being busier than ever working two or three jobs and going to school, life seemed to calm down a bit for us. Gram's visits home became limited to holidays due to both a decline in her condition and the fact I had to work weekends at one of my jobs. This change was hard to accept at first. However, I was thankful to be able to visit Gram at the care facility several times a week and to bring her home when possible. I still struggled with missing Nikki, but found comfort in Luke and Sadie's attempts to cheer my mood and in reading passages in the Bible. I came to accept that everything in life happens for a reason, and when we don't understand the reasons, we have to rely on our faith to see us through.

Things were going along pretty well when a coworker asked me if I would be interested in adopting a German shepherd puppy. Never one to pass up an opportunity to help a dog or to work with a German shepherd, I agreed. Bo came to stay with us in January of 2012. I thought adopting him would be like my experiences with Nikki and Sadie, but things were very different with Bo.

After about a year with us, Bo became very ill. His illness was different in that it was of a mental nature and not a physical one. I exhausted all resources trying to get him help. While watching him sleep at night, I prayed for an answer or a cure. Bo was a handsome dog with perfect markings and huge sparkling eyes. At times, it was as if I was staring into the wonder lust of a teenage boy full of energy who was not quite sure what to do with it all. My heart ached for him because he showed potential, but he could not maintain any level of understanding. In March of 2013, Bo's condition worsened exponentially.

Chapter Sixteen

Goodbye Again, Hello My Friend

"Lisa, you can't go on like this. We've done what we could, but I'm afraid there is no cure for Bo's condition. I'm sorry, but the safety of everyone is at stake here. We are going to have to make a difficult decision," Dr. Ken explained as we stood in his office after Bo's latest incident.

"I understand and agree. There is only one safe place for Bo," I whispered while holding back tears. I did not want to let go, yet I could not hold on due to the severity of Bo's condition.

Kneeling down next to Bo, I took a deep breath and said, "Bo, I'm afraid we are out of options. We gave it a good try buddy, but this just is not working. I am out of resources, and this is the best place I can think of to send you. You will have no fears in heaven. Whatever it is that is wrong will be made right…"

Choking back tears, I looked right at him. He stared intently into my eyes, as if reading my emotions. Extending his paw, he placed it right on my hand, never looking away, as if to say he understood. Something in those eyes seemed very familiar to me. Trying to focus my vision despite the tears in my eyes, I recognized a sparkle that reassured me. Bo looked very serious and intent as he studied me. For the first time in a long while, he seemed focused instead of distant, and his focus was sincere.

Dr. Ken had to take care of another patient, so Dr. Ann came into the office to both counsel and console me. She explained that sometimes things happen in a dog's life to change their behavior. In Bo's case, this change put him and everyone around him at risk for serious injury. Turning to Bo, Dr. Ann said, "Oh, buddy, I'm so sorry."

Bo passed away in my arms in the early evening hours of March 25, 2013. Dr. Ann wrapped Bo carefully in a flannel sheet and helped me carry him to my Jeep. She gave me a hug and instructions to call the next day.

I found myself revisiting history to some degree, preparing a final resting place for a dog I loved. Though the details of the situation were different, I felt like I was going through Nikki's death all over again. Inside, the pain cut deeply.

Standing under the apple tree, shovel in hand, I contemplated a fitting spot for Bo. Nikki had been laid to rest to the east, for she was my sunrise and sunshine. After some thought, I started digging on the southern side of the tree. Bo was named after Bo Duke of the TV show *The Dukes of Hazzard*, which was set in the southern state of Georgia. He also had huge paws and favored his left front leg, like a southpaw. Thus, I reasoned his resting place should be to the south of the tree.

As I dug, it occurred to me that Bo was too young to know anyone in heaven. For a moment I panicked, thinking he would not have anyone to look out for him at heaven's gates. Then I remembered that Nikki's spirit watched over us every day from her spot under the apple tree. Crying I said, "Nikki, you are the only one in heaven that knows Bo. You are also the only person I know who can handle him when he gets there. Please wait for him and make sure he gets to where he needs to be."

Taking a deep breath, I went to get Bo from the Jeep. After gathering him gently in my arms, I whispered, "Ok buddy, this is it. Just look for the dog at the gate. She'll show you where to go. Remember, just look for the dog at the gate."

It was now dark, and as I rounded the garage on the way to the apple tree, I saw the only solar light on in the garden under the tree was the one next to Nikki's stone. *She was waiting!* A wave of energy swept over me. *He's on his way Nik! Keep an eye out. He's on his way.*

Kneeling down to the ground, I carefully laid Bo to rest with his favorite bone on top of him. Under my breath, I said "Just look for the dog at the gate buddy. Just look for the dog at the gate." Silently, I said the Our Father then stood up.

My parents arrived and helped me cover Bo's body. Part way through, I looked to the side and saw the solar light closest to where Bo was laid to rest turned on. *Okay. This is my sign. I know you made it alright. Thanks, Nik, for showing him the way.*

Though I was exhausted, I cleaned Bo's dishes and put them away in a cupboard. Entering the living room, I realized his crate would need to be moved. I took it apart and put it outside on the porch. Coming back into the living room, I suddenly realized how much space Bo had taken up. He was a big dog, weighing sixty-five to seventy pounds, and all legs. His crate occupied a quarter of the living room, but I never noticed until that moment. The house felt empty, and so did I. It was time for a hot shower and an attempt to sleep.

Before turning out the lights that night, I wrote Bo's memorial poem:

Our Last Goodbye

In the chill of spring,
God gave you wings
To fly away
To heaven's gates,
Far from your fears,
Yet still cloaked in the tears
Of those left behind
In our last goodbye.

The day you left
We will not forget
For the snow came falling down
To the thawing ground,
Creating a heavy blanket on the grass
That our feet had to pass
As we laid you down to sleep
Beneath the apple tree
On the southern side
Of our last goodbye.

Now you are watching over us
From the sky above,
Playing in heaven
With your angel friends
Waiting patiently for time
To take us from our last goodbye
To our reunion someday
At heaven's gates.

As I wrote, I felt the emotion of his passing, along with a renewed sense of Nikki's presence in my life. Though grief enveloped me, I could not help but remember the better times with Bo and his boyish nature that brought a different perspective to life, just as Nikki had brought a fresh aura to the house years earlier.

For days after Bo's passing, the only lights that came on under the apple tree were Nikki's and Bo's. Nikki's always came on first, and Bo's came on shortly after. It was as if God was telling me all would be made well, but His timeframe may not match my plans exactly.

Bo's passing made me realize we all have limitations in life. Some of these limitations are due to things within our control, but others have roots in areas only God can control. Although this was a hard lesson, I realized it was one I needed to learn, come to understand, and accept in time.

Chapter Seventeen
Finding Peace

Gram's condition grew steadily worse as the days turned into weeks and months. She started having difficulty recognizing me during our visits. This was hard for me to swallow, especially since I had been Gram's helper since childhood. Her short term memory was not good at all, but her long term memory on certain things was very sharp. The things she remembered well included her childhood years, her siblings, and the dogs. Often, though she did not know my name, the first words to me as I entered her room were, "How are my dogs? Is Luke behaving? How about Sadie?"

Between wrestling with Gram's condition, dealing with Bo's passing, and trying to navigate life's other storms, I grew very restless. To distract my mind, I gutted my bedroom above the kitchen and started remodeling the room. It was the first project inside the house Gram did not protest, and it felt strange without Nikki, for she had been with me through all the others. Sadie took it upon herself to act as the inspector each night after I was done working. Luke resumed his role as stealer of tools. We were moving along well when a phone call changed our plans.

"Hello," I answered.

"Lisa!" the voice on the other end shouted.

"Yes, Gram" I replied, recognizing Gram's voice.

"I think this is it. Can you come now?" Gram asked.

"What do you mean by this is it, Gram?" I asked in reply.

"I think I'm going to die and don't want to be alone," Gram replied matter-of-factly.

"Mom or I will be right there, Gram. Hold on!" I said, before calling my mom to tell her about the latest turn of events.

Within minutes, I was driving to the care facility. It was starting to snow, so I had to be careful. My parents and sister also made the trip. Walking into Gram's room, I was relieved to see her sitting up like nothing was wrong. We asked Gram some questions as the nurse came into the room. Gram had some severe pain in her chest around her heart. The nurse explained the doctor had ordered medication to help remove fluid, and Gram would be placed on oxygen to help improve her comfort level. All of Gram's vital signs were normal, so if the fluid went away, she would feel better.

We sat and talked with Gram until late that night. Finally, she said, "Well, you better go home. It's snowing, and I don't want any of you to get stuck or into an accident."

Too tired to argue, we left. The next day was a Thursday and Gram called me because she was worried the roads were too bad for me to visit her. Although I explained I could come see her, she insisted I stay home, so I did. My mom went to see Gram on Friday. Mom told me Gram was doing well, but had complained of being tired. We thought the medication may be partly responsible for how Gram felt and decided to try to remain calm.

On Saturday, December 14, 2013, I was getting ready for work when my cell phone rang. The caller was a nurse from the care facility. Gram had taken a turn for the worse. If I wanted to see her, the nurse suggested I hurry. I quickly called my parents and sister, who were on their way to visit other relatives. Fortunately, I caught them before they got onto the interstate. I called off work, gave Luke and Sadie a quick goodbye, and headed to the care facility.

Entering Gram's room, I found my parents and sister already there. It was shortly after 9:00 AM. Mom sat next to the bed holding Gram's left hand. My sister sat on the bed with Gram. Dad stood to the side. I knelt down and held Gram's right hand. She was having trouble breathing and could not talk. We all took turns speaking to her, hoping she understood we were there. Outside, the snow kept falling in large flakes.

Gram's pulse grew weaker as the moments passed. The nurse removed the oxygen mask to help alleviate Gram's struggle with it. The snow fell harder. Gram looked at each of us and nodded. Looking out the window, the snow appeared blizzard-like. The nurse asked if we would like to have a priest come to see Gram. We all nodded yes. The priest arrived to give Gram a final blessing. Gram clutched my hand through the readings. Her pulse grew even weaker. I looked at my mom, who was doing her best to compose herself. All of us were crying.

Gram stopped breathing shortly after the priest finished, but I could still feel a faint pulse. A few moments passed, and the nurse examined Gram. Nodding her head and biting her lip, the nurse said, "She has passed."

I prayed to Nikki: *Gram's on her way. Make sure she gets to where she needs to be.*

The remainder of the day was a blur of phone calls, tears, and decisions. Entering the house that afternoon, Luke met me at the door. He immediately sensed my sadness. Kneeling down, I said, "Gram passed away, Luke. Your buddy is free of her pain now."

Sadie climbed on top of me as I burst into tears and fell to my knees on the floor. We tumbled into a heap and sat there for some time. The house was eerily silent, save for my sobs and the dogs' heavy breathing over me. Luke and Sadie showed signs of restlessness.

"Do you want to go for a walk?" I asked them.

They wiggled and wagged in a frenzy. Snapping Luke's leash onto his collar, we headed out into the snow, which was now very deep. Passing Nikki's grave, I thought: *I can't believe Gram is gone, Nik. I just can't believe it. After all those years of struggle, she'll finally see peace.*

Returning to the house, I sat down to write Gram's memorial poem. Words flowed freely from my mind to the page as I replayed the events of the day. Filled with emotion, the tears also flowed from my eyes, running down my face in little rivers. Luke and Sadie came to console me with licks and paws.

"It will be okay," I said to them, "It will be okay in time. Right now it hurts, but time will help."

Luke buried his head into my leg as if to hug me while Sadie jumped into my lap. Looking at her, I saw a familiar sparkle in her eyes and had to smile, before reading aloud to them Gram's memorial poem:

Toward a Lasting Peace

As the snow began to fall,
The soul below heard the call
Of the Lord in heaven above
Saying come forth, come,
Walk with me
Toward a lasting peace.

As the snow continued to fall,
The soul felt renewed by all
The words the Lord had to say
As they walked the earth along the way
Into the white flakes like fleece
Toward a lasting peace.

As the snow fell,
The soul was compelled
By the presence of the Lord
Leading it forward
Through the flakes of white,
Past the sands of time,
Beyond the trials of days past,
Until in the flakes at last
The soul was set free
Toward a lasting peace.

Chapter Eighteen
Perspectives and Perseverance

The Sunday after Gram passed felt empty and cold. I went to church, but could not concentrate on the mass. Memories of Gram standing next to me in the pew many years earlier flooded my mind. Tears filled my eyes, and my throat grew raw. The fresh air on my face after mass ended was a welcome relief.

Relatives and friends called the house throughout the day offering their sympathy. Many of them shared special memories or stories with me. Some of the stories I had heard before, but others were new to me. By the end of the day, I was exhausted and glad to climb into bed with Luke at my side and Sadie at my feet.

Monday and Tuesday were literally filled with snow. The white stuff was EVERYWHERE. I put my bedroom project on hold and focused on clearing my head and making things more normal for Luke and Sadie. I felt like I was lost in a snow globe with emotions swirling around me.

Wednesday was the viewing. Entering the funeral home, I was surprised to see the Gram I knew as a child lying in the casket. She did not look sick or in pain. It was reassuring to see her this way, but I worried, for I still had no sign of her making it to heaven. I listened politely as others offered stories, condolences, and shared memories. During the break between viewings, I went home to let the dogs out. Looking at Nikki's grave, I fretted: *Nik, I'm worried Gam may be lost in all this snow. Do you think I missed the sign of her arrival in heaven?*

It was a late night for the dogs and me. We paced the floor together. Walking through the house, it felt extremely empty. Every little sound echoed, especially in my gutted bedroom.

Thursday was the funeral. I went for a run early that morning, hoping to find solace. Exiting the house, I caught a glimpse of the sunrise and stopped dead in my tracks. The color in the sky was the same as Gram's favorite pink sweater. I knew the color well, for I had seen Gram wear it all my life and had washed it more times than I could count. Around the pink core was a cantaloupe veil, just like Gram's favorite blouse.

A surge of energy rushed through me. "She made it, Nik! She made it!" I yelled as I ran down the driveway and along the road to watch the colors in the sky unfold. In my mind, I imagined Nikki meeting Gram at heaven's gates with her tail wagging, ears straight up, and eyes sparkling with happiness. I also envisioned

Gram's gray eyes filled with tears behind her glasses as she smiled to meet God and Nikki with Ginger, Princess, and Bo running in circles around them.

The colors in the sky warmed me despite the cold temperatures. As I ran, I watched the pink and cantaloupe shades morph into variations of other colors. The sky made me feel as if God was speaking to me through the colors and in the nature that surrounded me along my run.

Returning home, I burst through the door to hug Luke and Sadie. They looked at me a bit strange when I said, "She made it, guys. Gram made it to heaven!"

After taking a shower and changing clothes, I headed to the funeral home for one last view of Gram. Saying goodbye is never easy, especially to those whom you have known all your life. However, I was glad Gram was at peace, so the circumstances made this goodbye a little easier to accept.

The days after laying Gram to rest were a blur of paperwork, more decisions, and cleaning out closets. Though Gram had not actually lived in the house for the last years of her life, I felt an extra pang of emptiness. To rid myself of the emotional ache, I worked on finishing my bedroom project. Luke and Sadie did their part to add comedy and a little drama to the situation.

There were days when things went well, and other times when nothing seemed to go right. Life was going to move on no matter how I felt inside, so I needed to rely on faith to accept the present in order to have hope for the future. Doing so made me realize the extent of God's love, the same love that created the many blessings granted to me, and the same love that put trials and tribulations in my life so that I may fully experience life.

Some blessings are hidden in the beauty of the sun, moon, stars, clouds, rain, and relationships we have with others. Other blessings come in the form of pain, frustration, anxiety, and obstacles placed before us. Viewing these blessings as good or bad does not change the value of their worth or the power of their significance. Our view is not always God's view, and there are times we need to stop, look, and listen to what these blessings have to offer. On the surface, they may not appear appealing, but underneath resides a myriad of possibilities and potential.

Our faith allows us to see these possibilities as opportunities for growth, which provides us with hope to sustain our needs. As our faith and hope grow, we recognize God's love, which holds the power to change the impossible into the possible.

Nikki allowed me to find a deeper faith, for she trusted and believed in me even when I did not believe in myself. I always trusted her instinct, for she showed me she knew the right way. Our faith and trust in each other gave us hope and strength for dealing with life's storms, like Gram's stroke and mishaps with Luke and Sadie. In exercising faith and hope, we formed a bond of the deepest love, exuding a passion for living life in the fullest way—by recognizing the good in the bad and being thankful for what we have, even when what we have is minimal.

Nikki was and still is a great teacher to me. Her perspective on stopping to smell the roses—literally and figuratively—changed my life forever. The stoic grace and inner strength she demonstrated offered me great examples for dealing with life's varied degrees of experiences. She helped deepen my faith, strengthen my body and mind, and see a part of life I had been missing.

Thanks to Nikki, I was able to reach some goals and see certain dreams come to be. Though these things took time to occur, Nikki's presence reassured me as we waited together to see the fruition of our work. And yes, it was work for both of us, but we did it, and we allowed small accomplishments to fuel larger successes. We played off each other well, knowing God had made our relationship possible for a reason.

Although Nikki is no longer physically present, she is with me in spirit, most likely laughing at Luke, Sadie, and me as we make our way upon the journey called life. Nikki was a gift from God, and I am very thankful to have had her in my life for seven years. She came to me at a point in my life when I needed some guidance. She gave me all she had every day, teaching me to be flexible and to take things one day at a time. Her appearance and personality were remarkably beautiful. She was my little sweetheart, my loyal confidant, my helper, and the rock upon whom I built part of my life. She was a dream come true after years of waiting. Her spirit will always be with me in my heart, for she made a huge difference in just a moment's time.

Just a Moment's Time

It was several years ago,
But it feels like yesterday
When the world we came to know
Was forever changed;
In just a moment's time
All that had come to be
Was swept up into the sky
In the sun's beams.

The day will forever stand out
As bittersweet;
The world continued to turn around
Despite the melancholy
And sadness that pursued
The heart broken inside
By the truth
In just a moment's time
Like a drop of water in the sea
Moving on with the tide
Making history.

Though the years have passed,
The feelings live on
In the soul that has
Clung to faith in the dawn,
Forever holding dear
All the memories,
Allowing time to steer
God's blessings toward thee
For just a moment's time
More than once in a while
Bringing to the mind
Thanks for all the miles
Trod upon the journey
Away from yesterday
As the world keeps on turning
Through time granted by God's grace.

Printed in the United States
By Bookmasters